Tennis in Action

John Crossingham

Illustrations by Bonna Rouse

Crabtree Publishing Company

www.crabtreebooks.com

Created by Bobbie Kalman

Dedicated by John Crossingham
For Kevin Drew, who took a chance on me

Editor-in-Chief
Bobbie Kalman

Author
John Crossingham

Project editor
Amanda Bishop

Editors
Niki Walker
Kathryn Smithyman

Copy editor
Jaimie Nathan

Cover and title page design
Campbell Creative Services

Computer design
Margaret Amy Reiach

Production coordinator
Heather Fitzpatrick

Photo research
Heather Fitzpatrick
Jaimie Nathan

Consultant
Townsend Gilbert
United States Professional Tennis Association

Special thanks to
Bronwyn Ann Hartley, Beata Knizat, Julio Murch,
Jordan Tedesco-Blair, Oluf Lauridsen,
St. Catharines Racquet Club

Photographs
Marc Crabtree: back cover, pages 15 (top left),
16 (bottom), 17 (top), 19, 22, 23, 24, 25, 31
Other images by Adobe, Corbis Images, Digital Stock

Illustrations
All illustrations by Bonna Rouse except the following:
Trevor Morgan: page 9 (bottom far right)

Crabtree Publishing Company

www.crabtreebooks.com   1-800-387-7650

PMB 16A
350 Fifth Avenue
Suite 3308
New York, NY
10118

612 Welland Avenue
St. Catharines
Ontario
Canada
L2M 5V6

73 Lime Walk
Headington
Oxford
OX3 7AD
United Kingdom

Cataloging-in-Publication Data

Crossingham, John
    Tennis in action / John Crossingham ; illustrations by Bonna Rouse.
        p. cm. -- (Sports in action)
Includes index.
This book covers the history, rules, skills, and scoring of tennis.
    ISBN 0-7787-0122-0 (pbk.) -- ISBN 0-7787-0116-6 (RLB)
    1. Tennis--Juvenile literature. [1. Tennis.] I. Rouse, Bonna, ill.
II. Title. III. Series.
    GV996.5 .C76 2002
    796.342--dc21

LC 2002002280

Contents

What is tennis?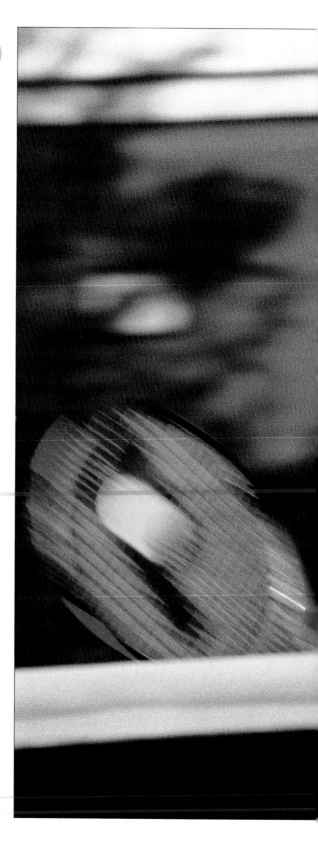

Tennis is one of the most popular sports in the world. It is played with a racquet and a ball on a playing surface called a **court**. Players hit the ball back and forth to each other over a net. A player scores a point when his or her opponent doesn't return the ball over the net or hits it off the court. Players continue playing for points until one player wins a **game**. A player wins a game by scoring at least four points.

Game, set, match

The competition isn't over when a player wins a game! A game is one of at least six games in a **set**. Several sets make up the entire competition, called a **match**. Some matches are played as **best-of-three** sets, in which the first player to win two out of three sets is the winner. Other matches are best-of-five sets. For more about scoring, turn to pages 28-29.

Singles and doubles

Tennis can be played by single opponents called **singles** or by teams of two players called **doubles**. Most of this book talks about the rules for singles tennis, but pages 30-31 have information on doubles tennis.

Grand Slam!

Tennis players often enter big competitions called **tournaments**. Some tournaments have over 200 players! There are many tournaments in professional tennis, but the most important are the four **Grand Slams**: the U.S. Open, the French Open, the Australian Open, and Wimbledon, which takes place in England.

Welcome to the court

A tennis court is a flat, rectangular surface that is marked for both singles and doubles games. The singles court is narrower than the doubles court, which has a **doubles alley** along each side. The court is divided in half by a net that is three feet (1 m) high at the center and slightly higher at the posts on either side of the court.

Different surfaces

The four main types of court surfaces are clay, grass, **hard court**, or cement, and **synthetic**, or human-made. Synthetic surfaces can be made of many materials. They are often found on indoor courts.

Serving and receiving

Players take turns **serving** and **receiving**. The player who serves puts the ball into play by hitting it over the net to the opponent's side of the court. The player waiting for the serve is the receiver. He or she must try to **return** the serve, or hit the ball back over the net. One player serves for an entire game, and then the players switch.

Winning points

In tennis, you get a point every time your opponent fails to return the ball. You also get a point if your opponent:

- lets the ball bounce more than once before hitting it
- hits the ball so that it lands **out-of-bounds** (see page 7)
- hits the ball more than once before sending it over the net
- hits the ball before it is fully over the net on his or her side of the court
- touches any part of the net with his or her racquet, clothing, or body

For more on scoring, see pages 28-29.

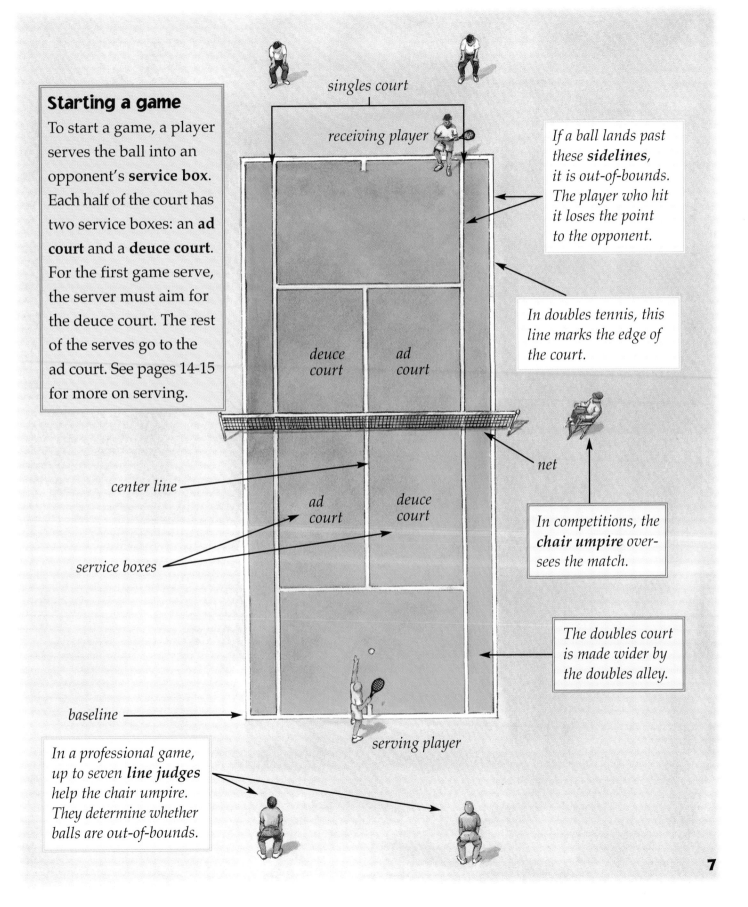

Starting a game

To start a game, a player serves the ball into an opponent's **service box**. Each half of the court has two service boxes: an **ad court** and a **deuce court**. For the first game serve, the server must aim for the deuce court. The rest of the serves go to the ad court. See pages 14-15 for more on serving.

singles court

receiving player

*If a ball lands past these **sidelines**, it is out-of-bounds. The player who hit it loses the point to the opponent.*

In doubles tennis, this line marks the edge of the court.

deuce court

ad court

center line

net

ad court

deuce court

*In competitions, the **chair umpire** oversees the match.*

service boxes

The doubles court is made wider by the doubles alley.

baseline

serving player

*In a professional game, up to seven **line judges** help the chair umpire. They determine whether balls are out-of-bounds.*

7

The essentials

When you play tennis, dress to stay cool and comfortable. Loose shirts and shorts or tennis skirts allow you to move freely during a game. In the past, players had to be dressed all in white. This dress code is rarely enforced now, but white is still a great color to wear while playing tennis. It reflects sunlight and helps keep you cool on outdoor courts.

Taking care of your feet

You'll run and jump a lot, so proper shoes are important. Look for shoes that grip your feet and have strong heel support. Your feet should feel well cushioned. The soles of your shoes should have treads suited to the type of court on which you play. When playing, be sure to wear thick cotton sports socks to absorb the sweat from your feet.

The racquet

A racquet is used to hit a tennis ball across the court. The **head** of the racquet has a wide oval shape. Strings are stretched across the head to form the **face**, which is the part that hits the ball. At the base of the racquet is the **grip**. The grip is wrapped with either leather or a synthetic tape to make the racquet easier to hold. Racquets come in various sizes, so before you buy one, ask questions about the different types and test how each racquet feels in your hand.

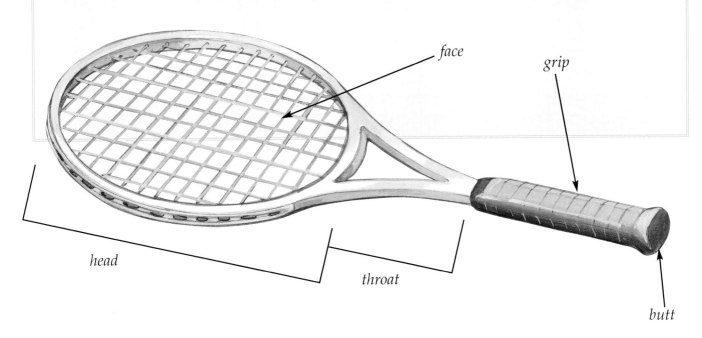

face

grip

head

throat

butt

The ball

Balls are usually bright yellow because yellow is easy to see during play. The fuzzy wool-and-nylon surface of a ball is called the **nap**. Air drags against this surface and slows down the ball. The inner shell of the ball is made of rubber and filled with air to make it firm and bouncy. It loses air fairly quickly, however, so try to use new balls as often as possible.

Extras

You may sweat a lot during a tennis match. Always have a water bottle nearby to replace the moisture you lose while playing. Sweat bands and a towel are also useful for keeping your hands dry.

9

Know your racquet

Before you start playing tennis, you need to be comfortable with your racquet. Get used to the feel of it as you try **forehand** and **backhand** swings. A forehand swing is one you make with the racquet out to your side. The palm of your hand faces toward the net as you swing. You make a backhand swing by reaching across your body with your racquet. The back of your hand faces toward the net as you swing. You will use both forehand and backhand swings to hit the ball during a game. Pick your swing depending on which side of your body the ball is heading toward and whether you are right- or left-handed. For example, if you are right-handed and the ball is coming toward your right side, you will use a forehand.

Get a grip

In order to hit the ball properly, you must learn how to **grip**, or hold, your racquet. There are several grips, including the **eastern**, **western**, and **continental**. Some grips are better for certain swings and **strokes** than others. Players switch grips several times in a game. As you practice the different strokes in this book, try different grips to see which works best for you.

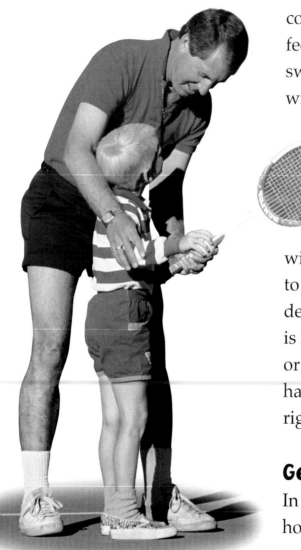

Some players shown in this book are left-handed, but the instructions are always for right-handed players. Left-handed players should switch "right" and "left" when following them.

Eastern

The eastern grip is useful for all kinds of shots. It angles the racquet face straight up and down, which makes it easy to hit a **flat shot**, or one that flies over the net in a straight, flat line.

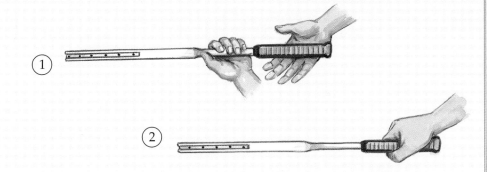

1. Grab the racquet in your left hand with the butt toward you and the racquet's edge pointing up.

Place your right palm flat against the right side of the grip with your wrist near the racquet butt.

2. Wrap your fingers and thumb around the grip. The "V" of your thumb and forefinger is in line with the racquet's edge.

Continental

This grip takes some getting used to, but it can be great for serves and backhands. It tilts the racquet's face slightly upward.

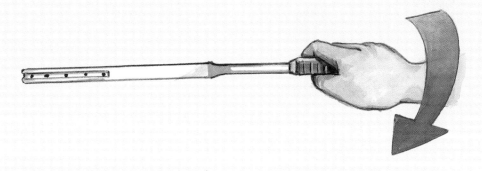

Start with a loose eastern grip. Hold the racquet steady with your

left hand and then slide your right hand around the handle to the left.

Western

This grip may feel odd at first, but you will use it a lot once you have mastered it. It tilts the racquet face slightly downward.

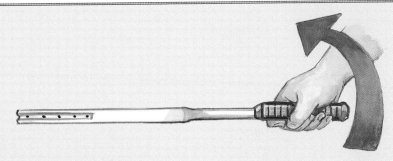

Start with a loose eastern grip. Hold your racquet steady with

your left hand and then slide your right hand around to the right.

Warming up

During a tennis match you run, stop, dive, swing your arms, and even leap. It is important to do leg, arm, shoulder, and neck stretches before you play, or you could pull a muscle. It's also a good idea to do light stretches after a match to prevent stiffness and to help your body cool down.

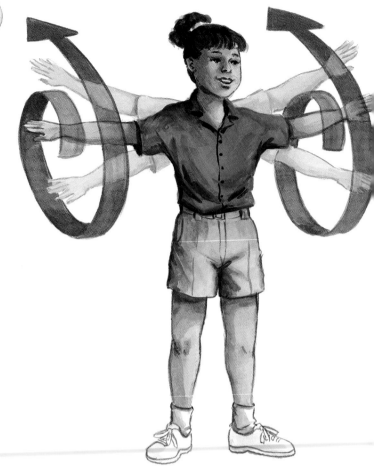

Leg crossovers

Stand and cross your legs at the ankles. Bend at the waist and slowly reach for your toes. Keep your knees slightly bent as you stretch as far as you can comfortably. Hold the stretch for five seconds and then straighten up and switch legs. Stretch each leg five times.

Arm circles

Stand with your feet shoulder-width apart and swing your arms in giant circles. Make the circles smaller and smaller. Keep going until your arms are straight out at your sides, moving in tiny circles. Switch directions. Start with small circles and finish with big ones.

Leg lunges

Spread your feet apart as far as you can.
Lunge by bending one knee and keeping the
other leg straight. Make sure your knee does
not go past your toes. You can rest your hands
on your bent knee or on the ground. Count
to five. Do five lunges on each side.

Trunk circles

Put your hands on your hips and
place your feet shoulder-width
apart. Keep your feet flat on the
ground as you swing your hips
around in circles. Do three circles
to the right and three to the left.

neck circles

It is easy to hurt
your neck, so do this
stretch carefully.
Keep your chin tucked
toward your chest
and slowly roll your
head from side to side.
Never roll your head
backward, and only
stretch toward each
shoulder as far as you
can do so comfortably.

13

Serving

Each play in a game begins with a serve. You get two chances to serve the ball into your opponent's service box. Your first attempt is called **first service**. If the ball does not go over the net or lands outside the service box, it is called a **fault**. Your second chance is called **second service**. If you fault this serve, it is a **double fault**, and your opponent gets a point. Bad serves cost you points, so it is important to practice aiming into the service box!

A good serve can also win you a fast point. A serve that your opponent can't reach is called an **ace**. It wins you a point even before your opponent can get into the game! To hit aces, you must learn to land your serve where your opponent can't reach it. Find a friend and practice serving to him or her. As you get ready to serve, pick a spot and imagine the ball landing there. Aim for spots that your friend can't reach in time to return the ball.

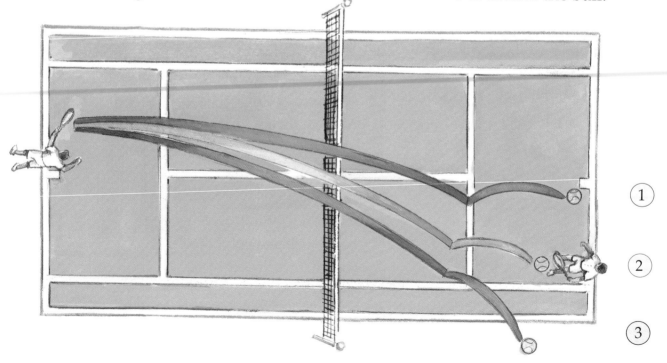

Serves down the middle (1) or to the side (3) of the court can be out of your opponent's reach.

*Aiming right at your opponent's body (2) **jams** him or her by leaving no room to swing.*

Under or over?

There are two basic serving styles. The **underhand** serve, shown left, is good for beginners because it takes less coordination to do. The **overhand** serve is faster, stronger, and more accurate. The player on the right is making an overhand serve.

The overhand
rear view

1. Hold the ball in your left hand between your thumb and first two fingers. Watch the ball as you raise your arm. Toss the ball straight up in front of your right shoulder.

2. As you toss the ball, bring your racquet behind your shoulder so it almost touches your back. Twist your torso to the right and bend your knees. Keep watching the ball as you start swinging.

3. Strike the ball at the highest point of your reach. Swing with speed. Flick your wrist downward as you hit the ball. Continue the swing until your racquet is down and across your body.

Returning a serve

When you wait for your opponent's serve, it is important to be in a spot where you can reach the ball quickly and return it with your best shot. For example, if the forehand is your strongest shot, you should stand in a place where you can use a forehand to return most of the serves. Where you stand also depends on how well your opponent serves. It is usually best to wait behind the baseline in the corner of the court to which your opponent is serving.

Coming in close

You do not have to stay on the baseline to receive a serve. If your opponent has a weak serve, stand closer to where the ball will land—perhaps in front of the baseline—so you won't have to run to meet the ball. It is also a good idea to move forward a bit when you wait for an opponent's second serve. A second serve is often weaker than the first because the player is afraid to double fault. These second serves are easier to return.

The ready position

As you wait for the ball, you need to be ready to spring into action. You should wait in the **ready position**, as shown on the right. Stand with your feet shoulder-width apart and your knees bent, so you are ready to move in any direction. Hold your racquet in front of you with the face straight up and down. Turn your body toward your opponent and keep your eye on the ball.

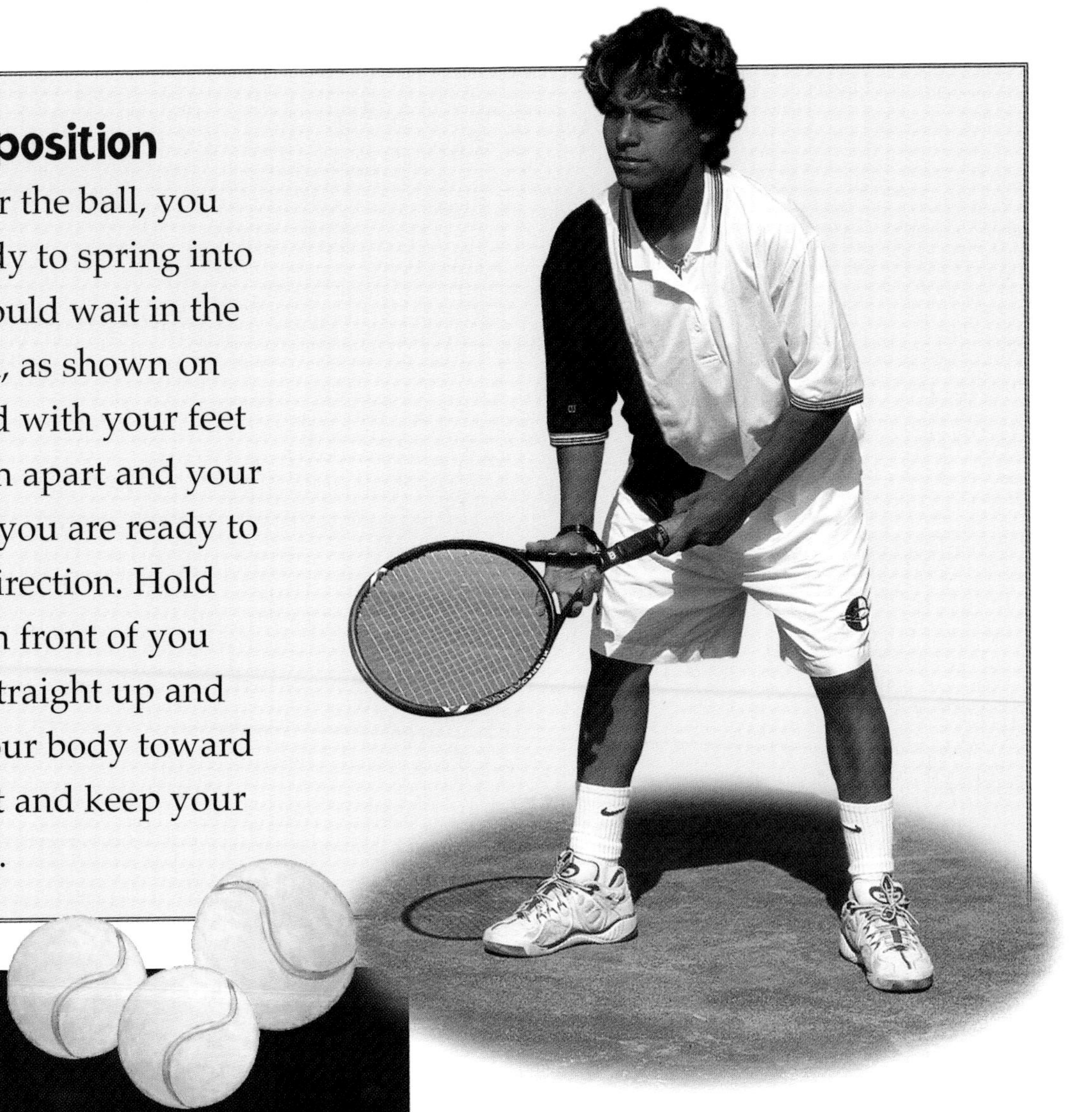

Ready for anything

When you're in the ready position, it is important to hold your arms loosely in front of you. From there, you can easily move your racquet arm across your body for a backhand or out to the side for a forehand. For more on backhands and forehands, see pages 20-21.

Rallying

As you and your opponent **rally**, or hit the ball back and forth over the net, you have to think about several things at once. First, you must keep the ball in play by hitting it over the net without sending it out-of-bounds. Second, try to **cover** the court so your opponent can't get a shot by you. Third, watch for **open** spots on your opponent's side of the court and try to aim your shots there.

Not every stroke you make during a rally will be a chance to score. Some shots will simply keep the game going. Others will send your opponent running and help set up the chance to win the point on your next shot. After each stroke, quickly return to the ready position so you can spring into action for the next shot. Keep your eye on the ball at all times!

Different strokes

If you hit the ball after it bounces, you have hit a **groundstroke**. If you hit the ball before it bounces, you have hit a **volley**. It is better to hit a volley when you are close to the net. Groundstrokes are useful in the **backcourt**, or back half of your court.

To add backspin, tilt your racquet head backward. Aim slightly underneath the ball and brush it with your strings.

To add topspin, tilt the racquet head slightly downward and hit the ball with a swing that starts low and finishes high.

Put a spin on it

Adding **spin** to your shot makes it harder for your opponent to return it. Spin makes the ball rotate forward or backward, which affects how the ball bounces. There are two types of spin: **topspin** and **backspin**, or **slice**. A ball with topspin falls fast and quickly bounces away from where it landed. Backspin makes the ball bounce slightly higher and slower. Adding spin can surprise your opponent, but remember that a ball with spin travels more slowly than a normal shot. This delay gives your opponent more time to react. Practice adding spin to your strokes and watch how your shots bounce when they hit the ground.

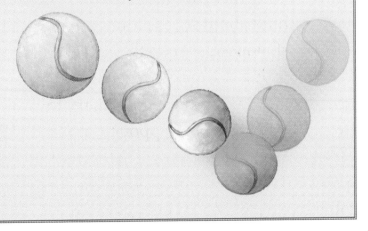

Practicing groundstrokes

During a rally, the groundstroke is the shot you will use most often. You can hit forehand or backhand groundstrokes. Be sure to hit the ball before it bounces twice, or you will not get a point! It's easy to work on your groundstrokes. Find a wall outside, stand about 20-25 feet (6-8 m) away, and practice hitting the ball against it. Let the ball bounce once before hitting it. See how many times you can hit the ball without missing a shot. When practicing on a court, picture imaginary targets and try aiming for them.

Forehand groundstroke

*1. Stand in the ready position. Rotate your upper body backward as the ball nears. This rotation is called **coiling**. As you coil, straighten your racquet arm and reach back but not too far.*

2. Step forward with your left foot. Begin swinging your hips, shoulders, and right arm forward. Keep your arm relaxed. Grip the racquet firmly but not too tightly.

*3. Watch the ball carefully and try to make contact with it when it is about waist high. Finish by **following through**, or continuing your swing after you connect with the ball.*

Backhand groundstrokes

Backhands may feel awkward at first, but the backhand groundstroke is an important shot to master. You can hold your racquet with one or two hands while you hit a backhand. Most beginners prefer to use two hands, since doing so gives them a stronger, more controlled stroke. Experiment with using one- and two-handed shots because each type has its own benefits.

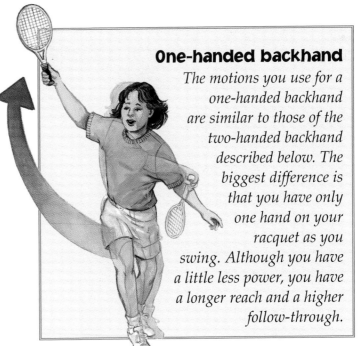

One-handed backhand

The motions you use for a one-handed backhand are similar to those of the two-handed backhand described below. The biggest difference is that you have only one hand on your racquet as you swing. Although you have a little less power, you have a longer reach and a higher follow-through.

Two-handed backhand

1. Hold your racquet with both hands. Choose your grip and wait in the ready position. As the ball nears, step toward it with your right foot. At the same time, coil back to the left and draw back your racquet with both hands.

2. Rotate your upper body forward, leading with your right shoulder. Swing your racquet in a slightly upward motion. Make contact with the ball at about waist level. Follow through until the racquet face is pointing up.

Perfecting your volley

1. For a forehand volley, step toward the ball with your left foot and coil to the right. Hold the racquet even with your right shoulder.

2. Hit the ball just in front of your body and follow through only until the ball leaves the racquet.

A volley is hit before the ball has a chance to bounce. It is usually hit near the net, but you can't just run up to the net and hope to volley. Your opponent will likely blast the ball right past you while you're still on the move. You should set up a chance to volley with an **approach shot**. An approach shot is a well-aimed groundstroke that sends the ball to the corner farthest from your opponent. While your opponent runs for the ball, you have time to get to the net for your next shot—the volley.

The benefits

You have to think fast to plan your volley, but it's worth it. Being able to hit good volleys allows you to use the whole court and send your opponent scrambling after the ball.

Easy does it

Unlike groundstrokes, volleys require little swing or follow-through. When you hit a volley, try to imagine catching the ball with your racquet. If you meet the ball properly, it will bounce off your racquet strings with enough force to fly back over the net.

Backhand volley

You can hit a backhand volley using one or two hands. Since volleying happens so quickly, however, most players use the one-handed volley. It is faster to get one hand into the correct grip than two. Try a continental grip for backhand volleys. It may feel awkward at first, but once you get used to it, you will have better control of your volleys.

1. Wait in the ready position. Step toward the ball with your right foot and coil to the left. Your racquet is even with your left shoulder.

2. Meet the ball just in front of your body with your racquet facing forward. Follow through only until the ball leaves the racquet.

Solo volley drill

A great way to sharpen your volleying skills is by hitting a ball off a wall. Stand about 10-15 feet (3-4.5 m) away and hit the ball at the wall. When the ball comes back, try to hit it before it bounces. See how many times you can volley the ball off the wall before it hits the ground. Switch sides to practice both forehand and backhand volleys.

Drops, lobs, and overheads

Sometimes you need more than a normal volley or groundstroke to get you out of trouble or help you win the point. In these situations, you can use one of the more unusual strokes. Practice **drop shots**, **lobs**, and **overheads** and make them your special weapons. If you use them wisely, these strokes can end rallies by winning you points.

For both forehand and backhand lobs, bend your knees more than you would normally, and bring your racquet back to a lower position. Swing up to hit the ball with the racquet tilted back and follow through fully. The ball should move in a high arc.

The lob

The lob is a high, arcing shot that takes a long time to land. It has two important uses. First, when you end up in a bad spot on the court, shooting a high **defensive** lob can buy you enough time to move to a better spot while your opponent waits for the ball to come down. Second, if your opponent is at the net waiting to volley, you can send an **offensive** lob right over his or her head, far out of reach. Although lobs are useful when you are in trouble, do not overuse them. They are difficult to control.

1. Bring the racquet behind your head and point your other hand at the ball. Take short steps to get under the ball, with your body facing the sidelines.

2. Wait until the ball is just in front of you and at the top of your reach. Swing upward and smash the ball. Follow through toward the ground.

The overhead

The overhead, or **smash**, is a powerful stroke that allows you to slam the ball into your opponent's court. You can use it when your opponent's lob does not travel high enough to be out of your reach. Timing an overhead is important. You should also be careful not to "overdo" it. Many players get so caught up in the excitement of smashing the ball that they send it flying out of the court or straight into the net. Calmly wait for the right moment, smash the ball, and follow through.

The drop shot

A drop shot falls quickly just after clearing the net. You can hit a drop shot as a volley or a groundstroke. The drop shot's biggest strength is surprise. Imagine you are in the middle of a long rally. You and your opponent are both at the baseline. Your opponent is waiting for another shot to the baseline, but you hit a drop shot instead. Your opponent has to run hard to try to reach the ball.

Disguise your drop shot by bringing back your racquet as you would for a regular shot. At the last second, turn the face upward. Brush the racquet softly across the bottom of the ball, creating backspin. Direct your swing in the direction you want the ball to travel.

Hitting a winner

Tennis is about sending the ball where your opponent can't reach it in time to hit it back to you. If you aim the ball well, you will hit a **winner**, which is a shot your opponent can't return. Learning to hit winners takes practice, but there is nothing more useful than being able to place the ball exactly where you want it.

Even if you can't always hit a winner, controlled shots will keep your opponent moving. The more your opponent has to run to return your shots, the more likely it is that he or she will miss one. Aim for a spot on the court that your opponent won't be able to reach, such as the spot that he or she just left.

Passing shots

The **passing shot** can be useful against your opponent when he or she is near the net. Every time your opponent is at the net, there is a small area on either side that he or she cannot cover. If you hit a strong groundstroke to this area, the ball will fly past your opponent and out of reach. There is no trick to hitting a passing shot. Just practice aiming your groundstroke, and do not be afraid to try a passing shot in a match.

Going cross-court

Hitting the ball **cross-court** can be helpful, too. A cross-court shot is one that moves across the court diagonally, out of your opponent's reach. This shot works well when your opponent is playing more on one side of the court than on the other. Instead of hitting the ball straight ahead to your opponent, hit it to the opposite side of the court. To hit a cross-court shot, strike the ball a little earlier than you would normally hit it.

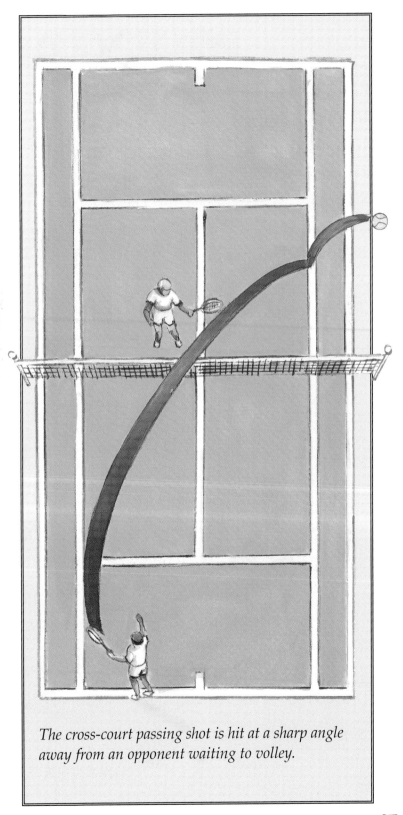

The cross-court passing shot is hit at a sharp angle away from an opponent waiting to volley.

What's the score?

Keeping score in tennis may seem confusing at first. Not only do scores jump by different amounts each time a point is scored, but they also have different names. At the start of every game, each player has a score of zero, or "love." The score is not 0-0. It is called "love all." When a player scores a point, his or her score becomes 15. A player's second point is 30, and the point after that is 40. When the player wins at least four points, he or she wins the game, so the winning point is called "game."

Keeping track of all the scores

Besides the points in a game, there are two other scores to keep track of: the games won in a set and the sets won in the match. The scoreboard below shows a best-of-five match. The five pairs of numbers show how many games the players won in each set.

So far, Jones and Smith have each won two sets in this match. In the fifth and final set, Jones is leading three games to two, but Smith is winning the current game with a score of 40-15. If Smith wins the next point, she wins the game and ties the set 3-3.

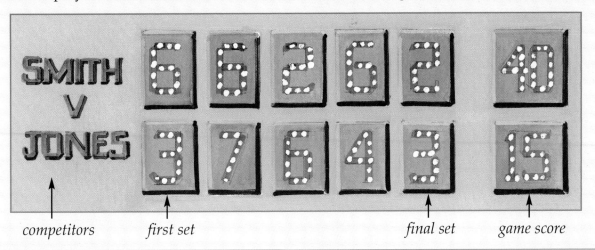

competitors   *first set*   *final set*   *game score*

It takes two

Players need four points to win a game, but they must win by at least two points. If the players are tied with three points each (40-40), the score is called **deuce**. At deuce, one player cannot win simply by scoring a fourth point. One player or the other must now score two points in a row to win. The player who wins the first point has the **advantage**. If the opponent scores next, the score becomes deuce again. The players must keep trying to score two points in a row.

Winning a set

Players need to win six games to win a set, but they must win by at least two games. So if a set's score reaches 5-5, the players must play two more games. If one player wins both games, he or she wins the set. If each player wins a game, the two players must go to a **tie breaker**. In a tie breaker, the first player to get seven points and be ahead by at least two is the winner. On the scoreboard above, Jones won the second set with a tie breaker.

Playing doubles

Doubles tennis is similar to singles tennis, but there are two players on each half of the court instead of one. The pairs can be male, female, or **mixed**—one male and one female. Doubles players must learn to cover the court and communicate with their teammates. Although there are two players on each team, only one player at a time can hit the ball over the net. You cannot pass the ball to your teammate, for example, so that he or she will hit it over the net for you.

Serving in doubles

Teams take turns serving a game. Teammates also alternate within the team. For example, if you serve one game, one of your opponents will serve the next one. When it is your team's serve again, your partner will serve.

Who plays where?

The player who isn't serving stands near the net. Once the ball is in play, both players can go wherever they wish. To avoid confusion—and crashes—it is a good idea for one player to call out that he or she is going for the ball. Both players should stay fairly close to the net and fairly close to one another. They work as a team to cover the whole court.

A server in doubles often stands farther away from the center line than a server in singles would stand. While the server above moves forward into position after the serve, his teammate covers the other side of the court.

Choose your side

Before a set, teammates decide which service box they want to cover—the deuce court (or forehand side) or the ad court (or backhand side). Once they choose, each player can receive serves only in that court. So if you choose the deuce court, you cannot receive an ad court serve for the whole set. Only your teammate can receive serves in that court. You and your partner can switch courts for the next set.

Don't go for every shot in doubles. You may move out of position and leave part of the court open. Work with your partner to keep your opponents from scoring.

Glossary

Note: Boldfaced words defined in the text may not appear in the glossary.

backhand Describing a shot made with the racquet across your body

coil To rotate your shoulders, chest, and hips backward in preparation for a shot

court The flat, rectangular surface on which tennis is played

cover To move around the court so that no areas are left unguarded

defensive Describing a shot meant to keep an opponent from scoring

doubles Tennis played by teams of two players

forehand Describing a shot made with the racquet out to your side

game The shortest part of a tennis competition, in which a player needs at least four points to win

grip (1) the handle of a racquet; (2) the way in which you hold your racquet

groundstroke A shot made by hitting the ball after it bounces once

match A tennis competition made up of several sets

offensive Describing an attacking shot meant to score a point

open Describing an unguarded area on the court

rally A series of shots hit back and forth by tennis players until one scores a point

set One part of a tennis competition, which is made up at least six games

singles Tennis played by single opponents

stroke A shot that sends the ball over the net

volley A shot made by hitting the tennis ball before it bounces

Index

1 2 3 4 5 6 7 8 9 0 Printed in the U.S.A. 1 0 9 8 7 6 5 4 3 2